SONG & ERROR

POEMS BY AVERILL CURDY

FARRAR STRAUS GIROUX : : : : : : : : : : : : : : : : :

SONG **&** **ERROR**

: NEW YORK

Farrar, Straus and Giroux

18 West 18th Street, New York 10011

Printed in the United States of America

First edition, 2013

Library of Congress Cataloging-in-Publication Data

Curdy, Averill.

Song & error / Averill Curdy. — 1st ed.

p. cm.

Poems.

Includes bibliographical references.

ISBN 978-0-374-28061-1 (hardcover : alk. paper)

I. Title. II. Title: Song and error.

PS3603.U74S56 2013

811'.6—dc22

2012021668

Designed by Quemadura

www.fsgbooks.com

www.twitter.com/fsgbooks

www.facebook.com/fsgbooks

1 3 5 7 9 10 8 6 4 2

FOR MY FATHER

AND TO THE MEMORY

OF MY MOTHER

CONTENTS

SONG & ERROR

SPARROW TRAPPED IN THE AIRPORT

Never the bark and abalone mask
Cracked by storms of a mastering god,
Never the gods' favored glamour, never
The pelagic messenger bearing orchards
In its beak, never allegory, not wisdom
Or valor or cunning, much less hunger
Demanding vigilance, industry, invention,
Or the instinct to claim some small rise
Above the plain and from there to assert
The song of another day ending;
Lentil-brown, uncounted, overlooked
In the clamorous public of the flock
So unlikely to be noticed here by arrivals,
Faces shining with oils of their many miles,
Where it hops and scratches below
The baggage carousel and lights too high,
Too bright for any real illumination,
Looking more like a fumbled punch line
Than a stowaway whose carriage
Recalls how lightly we once traveled.

COMMUTE

So her glassed, gold-vermeiled eye won't burn up
In light; so she doesn't blink and lose her quarry,
    She who hunts by night closes her extra eyelid.
That membrane lucent as a veil of marble chiseled,
    Then ground with seven degrees of stone, so the veil
Appears to float, riding the tidal breaths of this,
    Last hour of night, first hour of day, Hour of the Goat,
When through my sleep light penetrates, portends.
    Sound: I dream the news—barking headlines forged
With song, *C'mon over here from over there, girl—*
    And wake, chased, into the publicity of morning.
My minimal devotions. Three times, for contacts,
    Teeth, mascara, I bow to the basin and I do not think,
Do not ask that this short day make even as much of me
    As my mirror. That the secret ministry of satellites
Dream no more for me this snow falling overnight.
    Or, as the watchdogs of work's false urgencies rise,
That running out, wet-haired, late to catch my bus,
    I might remember something like the wonder
Of those six children, in their new snow at dawn
    Shot from hills above a city smoked in winter frost.

Come on over here from over there. How far
  Outside I am the starling drift of children's play.
Aimlessness of one, gathering intent as another,
  Then another join (give) in to the urge, almost
Carnal, to trespass the soft, astonished surface.
  Did it (does it?) hurt too much only to look?
Like a rumor, all day they'll shadow my agendas,
  Meetings, lunch, strategic plans, when mothers cry them
Home to wrap them one time more against the cold.
  Citizen, again, of the bus, its tired democracy,
Which grinds down streets dour as hospital wards,
  Snows heaped like soiled sheets, I dream I might
Recapture that prior integrity, of feeling joined to act,
  Replacing this—this strobing incoherence, like
Televisions glimpsed through naked windows.
  Neon coxcombs beetling the hill's black brow
Announce in large red simple letters WONDER,
  Fortified bread of children and the poor. We're so close
The yeast I smell could be our bodies' own. But this,
  The salt of our unleavened selves, only sharpens
Twilight thirsts, for a tumbler's heft, or anodyne
  Of books where murder asks so little of my witness.
Over here . . . over . . . girl, my neighbor's humming
  As we pass, passing through red effulgences
Of snow that sift above the day shift driving home.

HARDWARE

You lean disconsolate on your stool,

                Sullen and certain

As minor royalty rusticated to this
Unhelpful climate of solvents, gaskets, pliers, and bolts.

Because they are new and manifold and useful

You feel their whispers against you. The staunch
Resistance of objects. How can I tell you

                my soul,

To exhaust the realm of the possible when

                Ever the light
Is uncongenial as February and your hand unlovely?

Like a dog nearly annihilated by nerves
And boredom chewing her paw to sore, red velvet,

You've torn your nails so far flesh swells
Closed around each bed like an eyeless socket.

Fingers inarticulate as moles nudge a debris
Of dimes not thick enough to hide

The Kool-Aid-colored butterfly flaring
Across the tender, veined delta of your hand

That heralds indelibly the eviction
                    Of our sad and vulgar flesh

With one word needled in black, knuckle-Gothic
                    Rapture

VISITING THE LARGEST

LIVE RATTLESNAKE EXHIBIT

IN NORTH AMERICA

First, silence. Then a single fly, the noise
Of a terrible patience rubbing its hands
Together, before talk radio's tiny rantings
Start to bleed from cars nosing into the lot.
Another day, another dolor. For 100 miles
In any direction this homemade splendor,
Built with the old West's ruinous hope
Something might be wrung from land
That promises so much, yet yields so little,
Plus the termite enthusiasm of convicts
Illuminating saints' lives on handkerchiefs,
Provides the only destination, discounting
The four dismal burros at Jackassic Park
Over an hour ago. Though none of this
Travels the distance needed to explain why
You and I have passed these moments accepting

The dark gratefully, letting our noses forget
That so many nocturnal predators together
Smell like a stranger on our parents' pillow.
Scorpions, black-licorice vinegarroons,
A fist-sized blond tarantula stepping
Deliberate as a muscle-bound bodybuilder
Share fractions of a rattlesnake's long power
To fascinate. Before lit vitrines we stand
Like the Royal Society's frock-coated members
Marveling over reports from the New World:
Of rattlers' loathsome matings and appalling
Beauty, of a victim's boot killing two more
Men until the *ominous tooth* was pulled
From its leather, of men seized by sorrow
Before the snake could be seen or heard,
And pit vipers so sentient they stared back
At men and marveled, tails shaking until
They seemed a vapor. What do we know
Better? The sky outside is hot, cloudless,
The blue out of which disaster strikes.
Relieved to laugh at the rattler's habitat
In *mountains, woods, and desserts*, inheritors
Of this anxious paradise, votively we cluster
      In the dark.

OVID IN AMERICA

George Sandys (1578–1644), translator of Ovid's
Metamorphosis English'd, Mythologized, and Represented
in Figures, *and resident treasurer of the Virginia Company
for its settlement at Jamestown (1621–1624)*

I. A LONG VOYAGE, 1621

I left you, Thomas, where you are:
A humming late summer afternoon
& mottled by shade a man reading a letter
Becomes the image of a man reading
That I am forgetting.
This page is small yet stout enough
To bear me whole upon it to you
All the way in London. I may expand
Myself at leisure then fold it tight,
A sanctuary;
Like our vessel christened *The George*,
My letter is another ark to preserve me: George.

No midnight is so private as the sea's:
Timbers breathe, a loose rope snaps, & as the wind
Shoves you behind then slaps your face,
Seeing nothing, nothing to be seen, you feel
Unhoused, evicted from time.
But tonight, my love, my lamp is feathered, shy,
Herald of the next ransack & assail.
Behold the storm petrel! Gray wick-threaded throat
Burning the oil secreted, an amber musk
Of uncompassed seas & the solitary hunt,
Of error & sign, &
That delirium—which turned
Our ship's boy to mowing fields of Atlantic salt.
Like windrows he dropped the waves.

Until gaffed, pulled like a sleeve
Through himself,
He will live, tongue-bit, torn.
To return likely to a stool set on the shale
Where he can mend nets skirted by braggarts
Who have never traveled farther
Than the smoke dribbling from their chimneys.
I try never to imagine drowning.
Noisy urgent inefficiencies above, waves
Pummeling, sky shredding & the body

Anchored only in its just longing for air.
The tighter death's embrace, the more langorous
The moment. So this boy suffered
Some vast charity of sight.
He was what he saw, an adam.

Now he may be adamant & stain & distance;
& also that small satin interruption
Of terror—the instant breath's
Orphaned by self's perishing through poetry.
Like Daphne his voice is forfeit for the song,
But we do not grieve for Daphne.

My bird-light gutters.
Its call had sounded
Like dry wood giving up a nail.

What is this your wound that you must follow it?
For you I had no answer; consider only the reveries
Of the carpet navigator in his room. Listening
To collisions of wave & star outside his tower,
Rock-rapt, icebound, with a mind by dread
& ceremony & the dozen arts of courtesy
Girded, he invented those ideal earths in latitudes
Unstrung that I now trespass—

After I had translated two books
To pouring seas & clamor of sailors
I began to brood long on landlessness,
Coming to believe it my sovereign, my home,
When on the flat horizon of weeks at noon
The flaw: a color merely, private, ethereal, collecting
Heft in the warp of time. Days
Before we quailed at the barbed illegible pelt
Of forest, I wrecked, forlorn upon its savor,
Sweet damage of apples
Fermenting in rain-soaked hay,
Giving way to something ranker—
I tasted it at dinner on my tongue.
I am His Majesty's servant as my God made me;
Also my damps & exaltations; I am afraid.

Heaven & hell enlisted their geographers,
A map has opened the soul's five hinges, & Persian
With expectance how often have I feasted
On departure. London, Naples,
Marriage, Damascus, now your dear person.
So much flowing through me
My sight has silted dark my mouth. I beg
All the many tongues your wonder cabinet holds
—Dolphin, mockingbird, Muscovy bear—to tell

This arrival, so unforeseen, disorderly
As my hope you will not forget
Who I was, & am,
Unwildered, unwestered, constant, returning.

Bless you where you are, & where you would be
When there, & bring you thither.
                              My love,
What may never not be strange? What,
This morning, will wake & make me new.

It begins like a legend told to a fretful child:
It was, it was, and it was not. It begins
As if with symptoms of that sweat
I hear, so late (oh not
Thank God too late), you were spared:
A little blush along the throat. A restlessness.
Then the silkworm's casement, tapering
& pale as the egg of a chimney swift,
Which we will convert to cloth
To cover the naked Indian. A bobbin,
Which dropped in my tisane would ravel the maelstrom
Of silk. Spindle of whirlwind, spoonful
Of follow. The thread's stained scalding mile
Pours out my glass tempered in our kiln,
As each new settler is also seasoned
In this furnace, our new-found land.
(As the man drowning believes he digests
The mild water, as the damned marry flame
& yet blister, so do I know myself
Grasped by change at the stroke of change.)
Hold this glass up to your eye & through
Its pebbled horizon you may spy your room,
See its ire of surfaces sore with chairs.

Green grass green grace . . .
Would that I could account this world one
Where nothing is lost, only exchanged.

Without coppice, park, romancely glade,
Or commanding vantage,
Woods press on us; they fester,
& they watch. To the northeast white spruce,
Phalanxes of fledging pinions, clamp
Root to granite & hoard
What they glean off salt fog, sea spray, & stone.
From ewers of willow oaks darkness steams.
At breakfast I have pinched the plantlets
Insinuated by a maple's winged seed overnight;
It unclasps twin leaves, pale hands
Loosening the soil of my rest,
They never empty of their solicitations.

I find no empires here, no apostles or emeralds.
Instead, all things a-broil with an awful begetting
& my hours unsettled by some new show
Of riotous & mystical imagination.
Though we might wish to wedge us barnacle-tight
To shore's edge, our foundation raised
On marshland recalls this irritable fact—

The estuary, a nursery of strange devices,
Throws off new forms so promiscuously
I wonder how the world holds any more shape
Than a dream?

From my hand at night (my light
Some oil in a dish or a rush taper smoking,
Not so different from Ovid's) flower
His fantastic shapes, shadows
Of an old empire's former splendor
Now perjured by Virginia's clay & leaf & sand
Turned to the king's profit as iron, silk, & glass.
Belief is possible at night, solitary, firelit.
Then, I can believe in Ovid's centaurs,
Or that he was met at death by a three-headed dog.
I can believe in your letters, Thomas, which never come.

It is for you that I persist
In translating fresh birdsong, like this bunting's
Comecomecome wherewherewhere
All together   down the hill.
(Where did they go, who went before us?
Starved trove: scatter of blue beads & a name
Grafted to that bald acre.
Roanoke.

There is my terror & my tale: to go west
Under this eternity of nameless trees.)

And what will you make of this
Humble hieroglyphic of nature I forward to you?
Nocturnal, double-wombed, variously called
Monkey Fox; Frosted,
Or Short-Headed, or Indolent.
Let this Leafy-Eared Rat-Tailed Shuffler
The naturals call Possoun
Join your zoo's other fantasies
& with the Little Military Learnèd Horse
Enjoy its dish of ale. Its fur is durable;
Its flesh wholesome, white, & pleasant.

With one hand I can reach for
A medicine man's last breath caught in a vial
Or a hummingbird, stuffed
With arsenic & leaves & looking
Like a fine jeweled dagger aimed at my heart.
With the other I brush away
The web spun in a fox skull's whitened socket
While a wild turkey glowers from its corner
Like a small dyspeptic dragon.
My cullings do not quite master my closet.

When I imagine myself returned to the smells

& noise of London, from my stiff knee

Sands grinding as I walk, no marvels

Except those which the mirror surprises in all of us,

The swan-white wing at my temple,

I do not know what to hope for:

That you not see me, or that you do,

But as though I were pinned under glass.

At my windowsill a quince widens

A jaundiced eye into the dark where are

Real nettles beneath the words & invincible red

Root of the madder.

As long as any image of this world

Sticks in my soul, I remain—

300 were murdered. Twice that
Refuse to garden, hunt, or gather food
But languish like sparrows sunk in a frozen pond
Staring up at shadows, waiting
The sign that will call them back to life.
They cannot imagine their future.
Haunts without words to tell their trial; like Io,
We would flee the noise of our new voices.

Last night's sun smeared across the sky
Its customary rose-gold gore. You,
In London, have applauded no tragedy
Your approximate heart might use to figure this—
This violence. The trees
Do not desist their manufacture.
The perfumier's corky bitch
Chewed out the tendon in her master's wrist
Until inelastic it snapped & back she bowled,
Off to the woods & not sniffed since.

With the smell of breakfast still in the air,
The aftertaste of lead was the scandal
Of blood. Bodies stung into postures,

Penitence, Weariness, Surprise, & cardinal
In red caps, red garlands of red roses
Wrapped around white throats, white
As bacon fat. None need travel any longer
For all have found what they sought:
Henry walks his own fields, Lucy is not afraid,
Will has finally grasped the subjunctive.
The dead do not look asleep.
We cannot sleep through this life.
I watch the flies at their devotions, & I learn.

Time will not end by water or fire,
But by a congregation of frogs who yelp like hounds
& ride each other in shallow plashes.
I am inhabited by things that wake me,
But do not show themselves.

One frog my hand holds like a swollen glove.
As your maid might pare a callus,
I trim the brief cloudburst of its brain,
Which has the texture of cheese under my knife.
The frog, insensate, blind as an idol,
Would sit until it starved.
If I put Ovid between it & the window
& tickle its hinderparts with acid, it leaps

Toward the light, avoiding the book.
Its movements finical as a rope dancer's.
Though she have her heart & liver pulled out
Another frisks & fidgets up & down.

Who am I so far from home?

A year——& through branches light comes,
A pilgrim out of March from a farther world.
There's a flaw in the air. I breathed it
From the swamp, a kiss of damp
Translated to a plague that would remote me
From care & corroding solicitudes, crown me
With this headdress of red-painted deer hair
& weight my ears with wheels of copper.
My face painted blue & silver, my body
Washed in crimson dye, they would greet me
First with lamentations to mourn my old life,
Then by psalms I could enter
Purged & reborn & singing in a tongue
Not mine *I know not where to go.* (I know.)

SONG & ERROR

For my mother, Audrey Richardson Curdy

It was 1986, when currencies to be changed
    Into multiple-launch-surface, antitank missiles
Swarmed through numbered bank accounts
    Like Ovid's *seething knotted seed of frog-slime,*
Which not seldome attracted by the sun falls
    In little frogs with the rain; when it also rained
Radionuclides, strontium, cesium, and iodine,
    Over river and clay, and over the poet's Black Sea
Exile, before the prevailing winds blew them all
    Across Europe from Chernobyl (jewel of a name
That means *black stalks* and tasted newly of metal),
    And I was in your room trying to build a fire.
Wet branches breaking: those were your breaths.

    What hid you so that at every hour's dusk
I startled on you where you lay, nearly resigned
    In the talons of your most personal shape?
Still obdurate, still wild as the horned lark
    Rising from its nest at the hunter's feet.

I didn't allow you to speak what I didn't know
     To ask. As far as the bolted iron door to adust
I could have followed, to watch the way
     You put on your flame like sweetness
Wearing the skin of a lion, and there kept
     My vigil mild while bones leached minerals
And cell walls ruptured. It isn't you
     Curled like a seed of storm-pine in a furrow
Of ash, but your same small jeweled hand
     Belonging to a Roman matron that I see,
Its livid reach from the black igneous rock.
     Too late to retrieve the truth, too late not to
Have been like the alchemist who, lowered by rope
     Into the volcano, feeling the sharp concussion
Of heat, reported his own eyes saw olive groves
     And sky, mountains, and rivers of water and fire.
What can I make of this? What am I to make?

ANATOMICAL ANGEL

L'Ange anatomique, *by Jacques Fabien Gautier d'Agoty, 1746*

Unfastened avidly from each ivory button
Of her spine, the voluntary muscles open
Virtuosities of red: cinnabar

The mutagen, and carmine from cochineal
Born between fog and frost—so many little
Deaths that Buddhists refuse to wear

Robes soaked in its thousands. Sunsets
Of other centuries fade in galleries to ash.
Red is fugitive: as the voice, the blow

Of gravity along a nerve opening to an ache
The body can't unhouse: as the carnation
Suffusing cheek and haunch like saucers

From the king's porcelain rinsed in candelight.
Gratuitous as the curl, the urn-shaped torso,
The pensive, brimming gaze of pretty

31

Postcoital thought she half-turns over one
Excavated shoulder. As if to see herself
In a mirror's savage theater as elegy

To the attempt to fill an exhausted form,
To learn again the nature of those old
Ordeals of wound and hand and eye.

THE PRESERVATION OF MEAT

Thomas Jefferson, September 1782

Dusk had erased the farthest blue hills
When he caught the low chronic fever
Of a fox running through the orchard,
And found the fox's windfall fruit, a dove.
With a small incision between its legs
He draws the intestines like straw-colored
Silk from a bobbin, following the thread
Back to the hand of his dying wife,
Plucked from where it lay on the quilt,
Glut as a late plum. His vision of her
Body, then, before he'd fainted:
A hive decocting its monstrous sugars.
Noting a fine verdigris ring corroding
The dark pupil, he sets aside the eyes.
Using a crow quill he forces a passage
Down the throat, into the body he stuffs
With niter, salt, and Indian pepper.
An elegy of tender violations: fingers

Spread feathers like petals releasing
The perfume of gunpowder that rouses
Him from his dream of work to surprise,
There, upon his own, the face of the fox,
Robbed, wretched, and cunning.

SEE THEY RETURN AND

BRING US WITH THEM

From closed archives of salt this one swam,
Salmon dying in the graveled stream—
A final notice stamped *Return to Sender*,
Skin torn in strips like last week's paper
Declaring the end of all change
In surfeit and return. An old aunt,
Palsied and widow-humped, it festinates,
Hastening slowly against tea-gold waters
Fringed by daisies of flattened go-cups,
And shattered empties like amber stars.

Like this, the evening's aqueous light
Gleams on kidney trays, rinses shadows
From nursing home floors: her mottled
Hand on mine, eyes seen far as they can
And blind. She labors to disgorge
The word, mouth opening, closing, opening,

Closing. A thousand silver tongues
Excised, the salmon die, violated, their
Animal privacies—and mine—compelled
To watch this long-eked ardor of return.

THE GOD OF INATTENTION

After the trumpets, after the incense
There were nights insomnia fathered gods
I then rejected as too angry or distracted,
Or whose appetite for submission revealed
Their own lack of faith. *Say our names,*
All synonyms for trust. Others spoke
In sugared paradox: *To know is to know*
All. To not know all is not to know. To know
All requires that you know very little,
But to know that little you have to know
All. And for a while, it's true,
I burned in the dark fires of ambivalence,
My attention consumed like oxygen.
I'd wake up tired, as I had with faithless men
Whose strictures and caprice begat,
And begat, and begat, and begat
My love for them, harvesting the same
Silence from my bed. Who listens
To my penitential tune? Accepts
My petitions for convenient parking,

For spring, for the self illuminated
Across a kitchen table, for . . . for
Fortitude? I've heard a voice, I'm sure,
Advising me to drop this sentimental farce.
Yet to hold the smoke of their names
Again in my mouth I'd resurrect
The dead, or adopt the gods orphaned
By atheists, except the gods they've made
From disbelief no one's faith could tolerate.
Refusing to make the same mistake
Just once, I've cried out to the dark
Many names, most given up routinely
As the secrets of friends. If you're a cup
Will my lips profane your own? If a comb
Will I feel your teeth against my neck?
If a wall I may be darker than your shadow.
And if a door I will unlatch you, letting in
All the little foxes from the vineyard.

CHIMERA

Álvar Núñez Cabeza da Vaca (ca. 1490–1560), author of
Naufragios (Shipwrecks), *which chronicles his six years*
in southern Texas and northern Mexico, including his
observations of native peoples he encountered, first as
their slave, then as a trader and spiritual healer

I WILL TAKE YOUR STONY HEART
AND GIVE YOU ONE OF FLESH.

The wake   sewing shut those white lips
and after   when leagues   and all behind to salt
fell   the grateful Spaniards prayed
It became their habit   to turn eyes   sore away
from surfeit   Rashes and abrasions of spring
leaf stem vine blossom aphid & berry stridulant
intricate and promiscuous   without the rose
or borage or pomegranate bowered
in flaunting silks on gauntlet cuffs   No
none of that repose their soldier love required to root

20,000 had died in Ravenna   He survived
without mark to show what he knew
how fear cramped each man solitary
inside himself until the spark that leapt   stinging
them on to violence   the grass-fire battle frenzy
the grass that kneels to its burning

                                    Then aftermath's
vegetable melee   limbs and bodies

But what is not threat in this contagion and panic
of green   Whores wives saints sovereigns
this beach   that thick-leaved mustardy shrub   Names
he thinks   the names keep slipping

Swift   intent   armored obdurate as beetles   no one man
felt the wound of where like Adam   too late he walked

                                  : : : : :

The air   flexing   began to bruise green around them
the fresh human injury of them   Like flies
trapped in a bottle   they didn't know what to do
and carried on doing it
while bird   by bird invisible rescinded its song
while the sun   a drop of vinegar in milk   curdled the sky

Quiet   sumptuous as pain eased but by what hand
            abrupt as that held in the breath
exhausted just before the witch confesses

Like an executioner   who ropes hair over hand
to bend and lengthen the neck for his ax
the wind brutalized palm trees   spun men
before it loosely as leaves in a stream
He linked arms with another
    Broken wing   Splintering oar   Chainless anchor
dragging through darkness thick with sand and water and noise
whistles braying drums timbrels & ululations
Pressed all night to the porch of the storm his ear
mistook the self's own alienated music   called it sorcery

That the fury never ended he would learn
walking the eye of its silence

After the hurricane the stunned brilliance   like a spell
or question he woke into   waking by himself   to himself
and naked as a saint   to discover his ship
    with its ropes tools weapons salves Spain
was the anchored ship
now hoisted on planks of sunlight   over the palm trees
sailing out of sight   The boat sick

for such mirth
made by root sap riverbank & squirrel
it would return to that green oak it once had been

: : : : :

In what hour of what night did he know his soul
to turn a stranger to him
Pilgrim   he will venture forth across uncertain fields
Explorer   he will cry out

                                    He may be nothing more
than a hide rigid with gore & soil to be
scoured pounded abused by caustics and by iron
and   in watered pigeon shit   kneaded until supple
for the hand—
                        but whose   and must
the hand continue to wear   or it will toughen again

: : : : :

Daily he marched his men into corrugations of
blue distances dissolving one to another   like promises
of gold & corn made by guides snatched from villages
As the Spanish found new ways to die   natives

loomed   naked on the horizon they looked

splendid & violent as idols   Their women & children

restored for ransoms of melons or fish

Often some chief would repeat his good friend

possessed more of each thing they desired   His noble gestures

spread like balm   his native speech intoxicating

yet so militant their hunger   his words came entire

& legible to their sense as the amber & musk that steamed

from these his fine furs

: : : : :

Cabeza da Vaca's dwindling force

through swamps & ambush labored   circuitous   stalled

like mayflies in their brevity & towarding and never

fable riches youth nor rest to take

                              Only the body

with its anxious extremities   eccentric   naked

not natural   from which a vein of fascinated shame

opened darkly   glittering   smoldering

like sea coal   Every eye interrogated

Each inquisitor humiliated

by these echoes of himself   his body violating

the silence

: : : : :

Now alone and exposed   approaching
he amassed his ocherous archive of blister
and of bruise   the old fabulous
atlas of faith in blood & smoke redrawn

Still even the most exacting map dreams
omits & lies brindled
                            with sums & suppositions

Every step makes him more wilderness
He goes interiorly
to trade conches sea snails & screw beans
for red-dyed deer-tail tassels and the arrow makers'
sinew & flint between ragged bands
surrounded by enemies   enthralled by visions
that command them to bury their sons alive
Girls whose marriages would multiply their foes
become meat for their dogs
Where were the jades turquoises zinziber Where
the sacred monsters cannibals or kings fielding legions
of dog-headed warriors
                            Husbands groaned
bucked by pain onto the dirt when wives gave birth

& both sexes wept
strenuously after any absence   overjoyed to see each other
again in no essential changed

Had any man traveled farther than he

: : : : :

Whether time is the ripening of fruit   the dying of fish
& the position of stars   or all
the king's clocks ringing his will upon the quarter hour
hunger is the self's severe eternal god
From desert skies could be harvested evanescing
bounties   dove rabbit wild boar mountain lion
when for two months the natives drank bad water
and ate only oysters
                              Or salamanders ants dirt
deer dung but also many days without
To suffer even this much
demands devotion   & the ingenuity of the wasp
which deposits eggs in the walking nursery of a spider

A single brief season happy to know enough
everyone was summoned by neat cornet-shaped fruits
the prickly pear   migrating north   as it sweetened

from parrot through orchid
What use ambition in the desert   or will
The pangs can shrink but never close

: : : : :

He came late to healing   Even a stone
they said possessed its virtue and how could he
as well so different from themselves   solicit less
Left within his heart   sealed   it might sour
                              They starved him
The power grew   Passed along from tribe to tribe
intangible economy of magic
increased by use

Fright filled some with a lassitude they withered on
others suffered cramps headaches   or had been struck
by a sorrow   a terror   a surfeit
Blessing each joint with a cross and that something
of him might be spent on the hurt
he breathed over it   Just a little game he played to eat

before his mind emptied   stroking down & up the air
like a kingfisher
under the shadow of the vaulting falcon that played it

When he lifted his hands   his fingers
glowed like ten lamps of fire   Why not be all
fire

: : : : :

How much can I change before I am changed
It has been years   so long
without abradings of any other to recall him

Dilation   digression   by these ways he will return

Natives said he could not be
Christian   whose eyes they felt crawl over them
as if where women & men had stood was
desolating space   His own people turned
away   warding off this apparition of a new fault
in themselves   This man

neither their stone houses
nor the need that stirs the fox's miles   nor the moon
following   which laid down his bones
to scry the distances in him   but as though
pierced by some small passive wingless insect
whose gall   blighting him

would concealed suckle & multiply its question
down a thousand generations
he was that

                  which they'd feared most to find
now abject   now famous

Twice a year his skin like muslin   pulled from his body
Without armor or felted wool or hide afterward
he was discovered now
small pricked loose & unpleated   opening
to manifold injury & errand

A channel for pain and a channel for hearing

NORTHWEST PASSAGE

Standing on this deck I have watched
Morning's first pale peach jeopardy
Of light flush alleys and rooftops,
Just touching my neighbors' gardens,
Until they seethed like the green smoke

Of a new world. On these sidewalks,
With the linden's melon scent twined
Around an untuned engine's blue carbon
Monoxide and Wednesday's trash,
I've looked for an authentic eloquence:

Frobisher returning three times
From Baffin Island, Boreal winds
On his tongue still, timbers strained by tons
Of fool's gold. Circled with lamplight
I've imagined sailing under discipline

Into strange seas where the sun hangs
Dumb as a cabbage all day in ice.

Even as sirens squall down the block,
I've fallen asleep in my armchair,
Tired as any theoretical geographer

After dinner, who dreams of trading
His knives for nutmegs, mirrors,
For cinnamon, pearls, and beyond—
Finding by brute necessity and skill
Some route between suffering and song.

ON A PAINTING BY A MEMBER OF THE

NORTHWEST VISIONARY SCHOOL

Like certain histories, this painting rewards
The glance away, as the astronomer's gaze
Can focus by falling sideways from light
That's captured in his glass. Its ground displays

All brown variety of horseflesh: sorrel and dun,
Chestnut, bay, and roan. Seen once it seems
Abstract as a map, rucked-up hills and plains
Laid flat and horizontal. On second look it isn't

Ground but atmosphere: our lowered clouds
And the constant, mild precipitate that's easy
To live in. A visionary's speculative geography,
Vertical as Chinese scrolls. Small equine figures,

Reticent as fetishes, fidget back, step forward
On leggy brush-flicks. Their rumps and long,
Elegant skulls are ash and bone, colors of myth.
When I number the amber beads of generations

—Dad-Grammer-Elsie—I enter that dove-gray country
Called the nineteenth century where one great-uncle
Turned left at St. Paul for Panama saying, *So long,
See you*, and my Scots great-grandfather greened

For the Pacific Slope and its old forests,
Smelling like the morning of the day before.
Not the place itself, but his idea of it outraced
The future with the pioneer's nostalgia.

The artist didn't paint the literal mountains
Of this landscape, its glacier-fed lakes, or cold,
Glaucous Sound, but a wild, original dream
Of it and a light that was already gone.

FROM MY FATHER'S GARDEN

From the green extravagances of my father's garden
You can see bare foothills, blue in the eastern distance,
The exposed roots to the long curve of the Cascades'
Frost-shattered granite jaw. Glaciers shoulder north
To south in as wild a white-crested array as any storm.
You can say the freeway sounds like an ocean,
Unseen as other forces marking this place, and watch
A pair of hawks cruise shrubby medians for roadkill,
Chased by a crow whose dyspeptic eye contains
The all of it: an embarrassment of grandeur in a wry age.

But there are landscapes we're born into like family,
Unable to choose, and these soundings and elevations
Leave their impress—as a leaf's fragile vascular network
Imprints stone of a younger earth—for more and still
More, the absurd white wedding cake of the sublime.
He spends eight bucks to send me a shoebox of produce.
To open the box that first time, to finger each vegetable
Atlas and almanac—sniff the dirt's tangy, suggestive rust—

Offers plenty enough: potatoes the antique, mortal colors
Of kilims, an orthodox minareted mix of shallots and onions,
And a squash's dark, chiton-pleated lantern, winter-hardy
Rind raked with yellow and tasseled by a dry, umbilical stem.

THE LIZARD

I wake to him—perched on my laptop
Like evolution's little scar he is
The digital evergreen of failing pulses
And midnight currency transfers, the ceaseless
Milt and molt of information. His elbows
Jut like epaulettes, and a sky-blue patch
Marks each obsidian, mordant eye bead,

Revolving separately as planets.
From his throat a pink bud swells
To a peony, offered strategically to threat or mate—
Gorgeous excess translated
From a foreign grammar of ornament.
Neither miniature nor minaudière,

Not toy or clown, but a philosopher-king
Catechizing the rough or honeyed skin
Of things. His head swivels
Imperially and he tastes the air, with the air

Of a man preparing to pick a lock.
But he can't escape his nature,
All zeroes and ones, void or integer

As god. Being, then watching,
Then gone, withdrawn to his peripheries,
He returns to that alert, invisible world.
I raise my sleep-numb arm and shed
Its thousand thousand scales, my fused bones
Lightening, fraying, to feathers,
To fingers—so starts the day's unraveling.

SINGLE ROOM

Years ago, I suspected I might end
Alone and imagined myself, fierce,
Stalwart, walking these beaches
With a driftwood staff. But not this.
In the one saucepan, which tilts toylike
On its base, I boil water for coffee.
To answer silence, I narrate the minutes:
Rinse the pan, put away groceries;
Between me and the Oreos I'll create
Dramas of temptation and resistance.

I came upon a sea lion, given up
In the dunes, inveigling scavengers. Flayed,
It lay gelid, flushed, freaked with sand,
At the crease of transformation—
Organ, orchid, odalisque. The gulls
Moved like sharpening knives above
A too-elaborate meal for one who eats
Alone. Behind the dunes, the Pacific roars,
Approaches, and withdraws, reaching
For something, for anything—everything—
                    But not for this.

FROM THE LOST CORRESPONDENCE

Constance Fenimore Woolson to Henry James

Cast out from work's absorbing converse
    I watch as men and women
    Hurry toward home, each other,
From my rooms in Ca' Semitecolo;
My grand travel's tin duenna
    Steams unheeded, unheard, behind me.
    Had you made your promised visit
I would have brewed that water you call tea
While you lolled on the divan, so oddly
    Slack compared to the discretions
    Of your chambered prose.
This last summer seemed a vestibule,
A foyer in which I waited to be called
    Into larger, warmer rooms,
    A season rich in patience
Passed in pleasant afternoons spent
Cataloguing the lagoon's lost islands
    Swallowed by the Adriatic.

I might have written histories
Of erosion, epics of incremental
Loss. By autumn my cochlea
    Had hardened to jasper, and I
    Heard new sounds, tickings and
Groans, small volute sighs, as if
Some internal balance had tensed,
    Shifting in the decline of those
    Immaculate days. Complain
As you will that in the summer
Venice is the mere *vomitorium*
    Of Boston, still there are dusks
    In every season where a conspiracy
Of blues seems to support all this Istrian
Stone (only in Venice does one walk
    On water). Those evenings one feels
    Almost exalted, clarified, this brilliant
Perfidy of illusion made manifest.
How light I feel then! And yet. My own
    True home, my country, I've found
    In your stories, dear Henry,—
Like your letters somewhat more satisfying
Than you. Although I begged you
    To include a woman who loved
    And was loved in return, it seems even

Subtle genius is deaf to certain registers.
If we do not root ourselves in others' hearts,
     our lives are spent on the periphery.
     That sensibility of yours is my
Predicament, capable of constructing more
From absence than most gain by presence.
     I thought I had succeeded in not
     Surrendering to empty forms. Resolved
Not to be the woman whose affections
Were incommensurate to the demands
     Made of them as I was not the tourist
     Conditioned to see Venice
As the atelier's empty vistas. But this
Longing, like the desire to hear Vivaldi again,
     Was the sliver around which
     My imagination festered.
Do I confuse you? My real city
With its odors of sea and sewage,
     Its workingmen and beggars against
     A backdrop of splendid associations,
And its image, the faded picturesque;
Love and the idea of love. *Basta.*
     I cannot live on these margins
     Overhearing imperfectly
Life lived in other rooms. You have

Such talent for arrangement. I should like
    To come back as a mountain,
    Something large and distant
Where people can rest their eyes. Distance
Makes large passions larger, makes
    Little ones disappear.

    I suspect I shall mean more
Later, that you will come seek me in the places
I have left, peering down at the stone *calle*
    From this casement (*my* periphery)
    To console yourself with a notion
Of madness, perhaps. How many times
Have I imagined you in my gondola: last night
    You were there, surrounded by empty
    Bombazine, merino, sateen shapes,
Reproaches of black dresses that you
Wrestled over the side, nervous still
    Of imbalancing. But they wouldn't sink,
    Kept rising, like pity, like
Horror pushed under, dark skirts belling
Around you in winter water like jade,
    Malachite, frozen milk.
    Make me a fastidious
Ghost in gloves and hat, and I will lengthen
Your nights, wading the eroded islands

Of your dreams through the entire,
Exigent image of a city,
Its many loggias and marble arcades
Flooding above.

Yours, dear Henry, Fenimore

THE FAIR INCOGNITO

Pleasure gardens, clubs, and theaters, fueled
by orchestras, move aloof as ocean liners,
impervious to those extinctions brief
as any promised by rouged women who comb
the pelt of men for one
peony-turbaned prince,
or Turkish guard in gaudy sky
blue and silver macaroni.
The little heathens of her breasts
tangled in the mesh of "surprise
pink" spotlights, she quickens, casting
herself away, spendthrift gesture
of the inveterate
debtor. For all the men
squatting in velvet tiers behind coverts
of smoke, she makes this show of secrets and appears
by everything she hides in ostrich plumes
or sequins naked as the marrow of the moon.

Imagination out-
strips event. Each patron

eroticism
is in the
mind of
the patron

believes she smiles for him alone,
gulled by the moth-wing deceptions
of her eyes. Shadowed with the washed-
out-bloodstain mauve of the garden's
iris, from their distance they look
like love's extinguishing pupils;
her gaze made to seem to
bluely stare unblinking.
All seeing, unseeing. The hunter's hounds
will raven him who tries to see more than he is
given, here, to see. As nature denies
itself no ornament, nearly thirty species
plume the girls turning on
their gilded stage, like that

antique cabinet filled with humming-
birds. Arsenic-pounced and dangled
from wires, they flashed sapphire, beryl,
anthracite, and twin spurs of red—
as though in flight, a motion re-
collected in tranquillity.
*Oh, that I had studied
birds*, Ruskin wrote after,
*instead of minerals; to hear the voice
of beauty in a hummingbird's flight, to follow*

their gaits and allurements, I might have made
myself something worth doing, done more than collect
those mysteries, which in
plain sight everywhere lie.
He never recovered from his
honeymoon, lying beside his
wife's monstrous body baring that
coarse nest smelling, too plainly, of
Venice. What names would he incant?
Honey-catcher, sun gem, black-chinned,
star-throated, trainbearer.

Would he have fared better
with his own Fair Incognito? Her flame-
stitched screens and fringed divan, arranged to direct dusk's
lavender-green luster to swell over
breasts and thigh, imply forethought, staging of effects.
Before she veiled herself
to accost Audubon
on the street, before revealing
herself so altogether un-
naturally composed. *Paint me,*
she said. Did she angle her couch
so viewers spied along her length
as though she were a telescope

penetrating mines of
unfranchisable stars?
It's known only that she corrected him,
his gaucheries of proportion and perspective,
the illusions of depth. A foot cramping,
or the slender arm offering us an apple
from a mason's thick hand.
Easier if she'd stood
straightforward as a caryatid,
her burden worn lightly as
a showgirl bears the migraine of
her feathered headdress, as though it
weighed nothing less than extinction.
To draw well, the eye must abrade
the line over and o-
ver again, not fevered
like the lover, but like the prisoner.
Until the hand slips the brain's snares, to move without
volition across the paper, leaving
the cardinal like a pulled thorn, or an egret's
fountaining plumage, or
this broken branch's bloom
of Carolina paroquets,
vivid and garrulous as girls

disappearing into the dark
door of a studio to pur-
      sue this beauty that is feathers,
      pomade, pollen of cosmetics,
         a birth scar masked by gems
         on chains so fine they're called
illusion; then to pose onstage wired like
a specimen. Bright gamboge, emerald, and blue,
    one parakeet lifts a detaining, or
monitory, claw; another, arterial
         red head swiveled toward you,
        beak opened, importunes,
      for centuries unheard, but like
      as life as any diora-
ma, theater of annulments,
theater of false consola-
      tions, theater where we must dress
      still to assume our part among
        the fugitive splendor
        of the occasions. Where
parakeets flag their dead like a flock of
carnations. Where revived in wax the conjurer
of the annihilated Algonquians
adorned by a blackbird, emblem of his transit
        between, dances naked

where, after, Audubon
took a walk with his gun. Before
age hardened his eye and he lost
the hand for drawing, before his
engraving plates were melted down
to build Manhattan, before his
mind fell into ruins,
the Fair Incognito
burned upon his inner eye, revolving
naked, wilderness turning into theater,
framed, foreshortened—that trick of revealing
what remains naked to the eye, invisible.

When I was beautiful

I was forgiven my raucous laughter.
                              Wedding guests
                feasting like wasps
on soft-skinned fruits and sweetened wines,
                even as a noise
                              more appallingly intimate
than thunder shocks some foreign air
into tiers of voile.
                              Leaves shuddering from trees;
                the body harrowed of will.
                                            My sister
was safe when I was beautiful.
                              I wore departure,
a jet's contrail, the initiate's reserve, a veil
                of salt sowed over enemy orchards.

Danger drew me because I was beautiful.
                              I thought everyone heard
the voices I could, calling my name. The dead
                needed me.

I've been so busy. So beautiful was I
                    my dress was the desert
where the ghost of moisture prowls
              the rooftop sleepers, where dawn is kissed
                    without heat and cities gleam
like pearls.
                    Jealous morning. Who stole
my dreams. Which took from me
                    old men and families
              strolling that unfamiliar promenade
as I calculated velocities,
              angles, routes
                              of escape, while
the truck drove into us, exploding.
              I believed all the experts, who said
that in her own dreams
              the dreamer couldn't die.
Put away the pictures—they never show the face
in the mirror. The sun was in my eyes
              when I was beautiful.

TO THE VOICE OF THE RETIRED WARDEN OF HUNTSVILLE PRISON (TEXAS DEATH CHAMBER)

Until wolf light I will count my sheep,
    Adumbrated, uncomedic, as they are.
    One is perdu, two, qualm, three
                Is sprawl, four, too late,

Night is already a thirsty county in Texas,
                Salt flat and unremitting
    Blacktop dry as my mouth,
    And your elastic vowels, my genial,

                My electric ghost, my
    Radio's lonely station. Because the spectacle
Of suffering corrupts us, all punishments
    Are now executive, offstage.

Most presume you a fable:
Echoes of approaching boot heels
That harry labyrinths of concrete corridors,
Or hooded in burlap.

We are convicted
As we are also pardoned: he cherished
His garden, or afterward he covered
The victim's face. You make no judgments

Yourself. Only in bursal tones,
Tactful as the file box
That shows, if opened, the neon, pleading heart
Of Jesus wrapped in barbed wire,

You perform penalties others have scripted, so
Untroubled by so many.
How long I have listened to you
For news of the opal distances,

Or rain to freshen the morning's arrival.
What keeps me awake? Nothing
More than a fly's dysenteric violin.
What puts me to sleep

Is your clement voice, saying
The dark has no teeth. While men like you live
In this world do I dream
I am either safe or spared?

EVIDENCE

It will be another artifact when found:
The wallet gone, of course; the phone.
On a metal desk lies the rest tossed
Into the vast, municipal ether, a static
Of things whose signal owner is lost.

One clove-scented, geranium lipstick,
Well-used, and a mirror, just big enough
To show a piece of face. Rain-swollen
Paperback, some place marked by a leaf;
Tissues; bus transfer; tea bags; pen.

A kind of story, though hardly news:

Will you know me when you return?
Sore and heavy with speeches, I lose
Proportion. It is better to burn
Than to last. Outside the ginkgo
Breaks its fleshy seeds on cement,

Still trying with that obsolete stink
To flag the mastodons. It can be patient,
But I have grown brittle waiting so long.
Even my tears, which I was saving
For the heroine's final aria, have dried.

Every hour is bitter. Write.

DARK ROOM

The camera obscura in Clifton Observatory, Bristol

We could be dead and this
Our little limbo. Where breathless,
Blind, cramped, we find
A table laid with the sterling world
We'd lost. Where looking back

We see what for so long
We half believed: people do
Go on. Go on. Beyond
The lens's range, a bridge
Is hung. We can't forget the gorge,

Or that other side where
Slaves bide within the old port's
Muddy shade, while poets
From those cowled faces amend
Their words. We postpone

Our leaving, rooted
By woods, an image
Of woods whipped into hilarities
Of green. Not the mottled page
Skimmed from planes, nor

An exquisite trick of the miniature,
This, though elm, oak, ash
Look fresh as any bouquet;
But the mind's own green clerestory
Open now to air. And the view,

A swarming hive of darkness,
Some unperishing, excited
Engine, without limit, without us.

NOTES & ACKNOWLEDGMENTS

NOTES

The title "Song & Error" comes from Ovid's *Tristia* (II.207; Loeb edition), in which he acknowledges two causes for his exile: "two crimes, a poem and a blunder [*duo crimina, carmen et error*] have brought me ruin." The lines of stanza 3 are quoted from George Sandys's seventeenth-century commentary to his *Ovid's Metamorphosis English'd, Mythologized, and Represented in Figures*.

The alchemist is Athanasius Kirchner, who was lowered by rope into the mouth of Vesuvius in 1638, returning to report that he saw a world much like ours inside the volcano.

On September 6, 1782, Jefferson's wife, Martha, died. After a silence of six weeks, the first entry in his Garden Book following her death is a recipe for "The Preservation of Meat."

The subject of "Chimera," Álvar Núñez Cabeza da Vaca, experienced hurricane, shipwreck, enslavement, and starvation during six years in North America. Though his route is disputed, he walked for several years in the area of southern Texas and northern Mexico. Cabeza da Vaca eventually made his way to Mexico City and then back to Spain, but returned to the new world as a governor of Río de la Plata, where his (relative) sympathy for the natives enraged his men, who mutinied. He was sent back to Spain in chains.

In a letter dated May 23, 1821, Audubon wrote to his wife, telling her of his (perhaps apocryphal) encounter with a woman he called The Fair Incognito, who had approached him on the streets of New Orleans with the request that he paint her portrait. When he arrived at the Fair Incognito's house, she threw back the veil she had been wearing to reveal "the most beautifull face." Refusing to give her name, she asked him to paint her nude. Rattled but needing the money, Audubon consented and returned each day for a week to work on the portrait. Each morning he would find infelicities of his work corrected by his patron. When the portrait was finished she signed her name in a prominent position and directed Audubon to sign his name on a shadowed bit of drapery. She paid him with a handsome rifle. The painting doesn't survive, if it ever existed.

Toward the end of his life Audubon suffered from senility.

The refrain of "When I was beautiful" is borrowed from Mahmoud Darwish.

The poems in this book touch on lines by John Donne, Ben Jonson, Ovid, and Pindar, among others.

ACKNOWLEDGMENTS

Thanks to the publications in which some of these poems first appeared, sometimes in slightly different form:

32 Poems: "Northwest Passage" and
"The Preservation of Meat"

BatCity Review: "The Fair Incognito"

Gulf Coast: "Single Room" as
"Single Room, Ocean Crest Motel"

The Kenyon Review: "When I was beautiful"

New England Review: "See They Return and
Bring Us with Them" as "The Salmon"

Orion: "Visiting the Largest Live
Rattlesnake Exhibit in North America"

The Paris Review: "From the Lost Correspondence" and "On a
Painting by a Member of the Northwest Visionary School"

Poetry: "Anatomical Angel," "Chimera," "Dark Room,"
"Evidence," "The God of Inattention," "Hardware,"
"The Lizard" as "Aubade Beginning with Sleep Apnea,"
"Ovid in America," "Song & Error," "Sparrow Trapped

in the Airport," "To the Voice of the Retired Warden
of Huntsville Prison (Texas Death Chamber)"

Raritan: "Commute"

Western Humanities Review: "From My Father's Garden"

"Sparrow Trapped in the Airport" was reprinted in *Pushcart XXVI: The Best of the Small Presses* and in *Bright Wings: An Illustrated Anthology of Poems About Birds*, edited by Billy Collins and published by Columbia University Press. "On a Painting by a Member of the Northwest Visionary School" was reprinted in *Red, White, and Blues: Poets on the Promise of America*, published by the University of Iowa Press. "Northwest Passage" and "When I was beautiful" were also recorded for Fishouse Poets Online, at fishouse.org.

I would like to thank the Rona Jaffe Foundation, the National Endowment for the Arts, and the Illinois State Arts Council for their generosity and support; I would also like to thank the Lannan Foundation for the residency during which many of these poems were written.

I am pleased to be able to express my gratitude to the following people for their inspiration, advice, and solace: Lynn Geri; Kimball, Jason, and Audrey Conlon; Robert and Dana Curdy; Richard Curdy; Karrin Curdy; Alan and Eileen Cross; Peter and Pip Murr; Danielle Chapman and Christian Wiman; Nancy West and Craig Kluever; Anna Keesey; Joanne Diaz; Sheila Donohue; Reginald Gibbons; Edward Hirsch; Karen Holmberg; Whitney McCleary and Joe King; Cliff and Deena

Guren; Mary Kinzie; Scott Cairns; Lynne McMahon and Sherod Santos; Robyn Schiff; Patty Seyburn; Shauna Seliy and Elizabeth Powley; Rachel Webster; and Leila Wilson.

With special thanks to Jonathan Galassi, and to Penelope Pelizzon; and for Naeem Murr—seven seas' worth of love.